UNZIP YOUR LIPS AGAIN

Ten things you never knew about Paul Cookson:

1. He was born in 1961 in Chelmsford, Essex. Luckily he was adopted very soon afterwards and brought up in Lancashire where he learnt how to speak proper.

2. His dad was a customs and excise officer who then became a farmer so Paul spent lots of time watering greenhouses, weeding potatoes, creosoting sheds and catching chickens.

3. The first poem he can remember liking was 'Daddy Fell Into the Pond' by Alfred Noyes.

4. The first record he ever loved was 'Cum on Feel the Noize' by Slade.

5. The first poem he ever had published was about his guitar.

6. Roger McGough was the first poet he liked.

7. The first poet he remembers seeing perform was John Cooper Clarke at the Preston Guildhall in 1977. He was supporting Be Bop Deluxe.

8. He published his first booklet in 1979 and a dozen more in the next ten years after forming A Twist in the Tale, his own publishing company.

9. His first children's collection was called *The Amazing Captain Concorde*.

10. He doesn't write as many poems as he'd like to. He spends most of his time performing them and has visited well over 1,000 schools.

11. He is rubbish at m

UNZIP YOUR LIPS AGAIN

Chosen by Paul Cookson

MACMILLAN
CHILDREN'S BOOKS

First published 1999 by Macmillan Children's Books

This edition published 2000 by Macmillan Children's Books
a division of Macmillan Publishers Limited
25 Eccleston Place, London SW1W 9NF
Basingstoke and Oxford
www.macmillan.co.uk

Associated companies throughout the world

ISBN 0 330 39133 X

Printed and bound in Great Britain by Mackays of Chatham plc, Chatham, Kent

Contents

Secret

Tell me your secret.
I promise not to tell.
I'll guard it safely at the bottom of a well.

Tell me your secret
Tell me, tell me, please.
I won't breathe a word, not even to the bees.

Tell me your secret.
It will be a pebble in my mouth.
Not even the sea can make me spit it out.

John Agard

Ear Popping

To blow your ears clear
hold your nose.
And with a POP
the blockage goes.
But please remember,
pay regard.
Never blow too long
or hard.
I knew a boy
who didn't stop
when at first
he heard no POP.
He blew until
his face turned red
and POPPED the ears
clear off his head!

Jez Alborough

The Recipe Alphabet

Ask for Bacon and Chips.
Don't Eat Fish.
Gulp Half an Iced Jug of Kiwi-fruit and Liquorice.
Mix Nuts and Orange Peel
with a Quart of Rice
and Some Tasty Underdone Veal –
Well, it's eXactly like Young Zebra.

Leo Aylen

The Tale of the Leprechauny Man and the Unsuccessful Fishery Expedishery

The
par-
tickle-u-lar-
ly
leprechauny man
tookle his tickle-tackle
and went forth to outwit fishes
(the water people).
Sat sandwich-munchily
on his tripodal stool
dangly into the flishing sterream
his sterring
sterrung from a hazel stick.

Unawary he was
that no hookit was attackled thereto.
Stared daylong at the horizory view
unawarily sating his piscine
(a bit fishy)
friends
on good delishibaitle foodstuffs,
to wit
worrmy maggits,
loafbits,
and wruggly squurrms.

When evening fell
(tripping carelessily over a mounting pique)
he meandered homywards
happy and fishless.
He knew that there must be a catch somewhere
but knew not where
nor why it was not to be his.
And after nodded dreamiwise
at his singing
crickety
hearthplace.

Gerard Benson

The Barkday Party

For my dog's birthday party
I dressed like a bear.
My friends came as lions
and tigers and wolves and monkeys.
At first, Runabout couldn't believe
the bear was really me. But
he became his old self again
when I fitted on his magician's top hat.
Runabout became the star, running about
jumping up on chairs and tables
barking at every question asked him.
Then, in their ordinary clothes,
my friend Brian and his dad arrived
with their boxer, Skip. And with us
knowing nothing about it, Brian's dad
mixed the dog's party meat and milk
with wine he brought. He started
singing. Runabout started to yelp.
All the other six dogs joined –
yelping:

> *Happy Barkday to you*
> *Happy Barkday to you*
> *Happy Barkday Runabout*
> *Happy Barkday to you!*

James Berry

Whose Dem Boots

Whose dem boots ah hearin, chile,
Whose dem boots ah hear?
Whose dem boots ah hearin, chile,
Whose dem boots ah hear?
Dem boots trampin down de road
Dat fill mah heart wid fear?

Gotta fin' me a hid'n place,
Whai, whai,
Gotta fin' me a hid'n place.

Whose dem boots ah hearin, chile,
Comin thru mah gate?
Whose dem boots ah hearin, chile,
Comin thru mah gate?
Trampin straight up to mah door?
Tell dem please to wait.

Gotta fin' me a hid'n place,
Whai, whai,
Gotta fin' me a hid'n place.

Whose dem boots ah seein, chile,
Stand'n by mah bed?
Whose dem boots ah seein, chile,
Stand'n by mah bed?
Waitin dere so patient, chile?
Tell dem go ahead.

Gotta fin' me a hid'n place,
Whai, whai,
Gotta fin' me a hid'n . . . hunh!

Valerie Bloom

At the Hairdresser's

"Crimped and furled, or waved and curled?"
"No, just a trim please."
"Streaked and greyed, or layered and waved?"
"No, just a trim please."
"A perfumed lotion, or herbal potion?"
"No, just a trim please."
"Brushed and combed, or washed and blown?"
"No, just a trim please."
"It's flyaway hair, would you like some spray?
It's ozone friendly. It'll make it stay."
"No, just a trim please."
"What about a new look, a whole different style?
It would only take a little while."
"No, just a trim please."
"Some sculpting mousse, or styling gel?"
Good grief! I'm going to yell.
"No, just a trim please."
"Are you greasy, normal or dry?"
"Normal! What's normal in here?" I cry.
"Just a trim please."
"Straight and bobbed, or a mohican spike?"
"Oh really, on your bike. Just a trim please.
What do I have to say in here to get the job done?
DO I MAKE MYSELF CLEAR?
JUST A TRIM PLEASE."
"Oh certainly, Madam, why didn't you say?
We're really very busy today."

Margaret Blount

Love You Batman

Love you Batman –
Love the way your batwheels turn
And the cruel curl your batlips make
And the way your cold blue bateyes burn.

Love you Batman –
Your dark shadow's on my mind:
The night the knight sweeps me away
For the dawn and broken dreams to find . . .

Love you Batman –
Let me kiss away your fears
Of evil and of lonely nights
And hard caped-crusading years.

Love you Batman –
Your firm hands on my skin:
Your identity revealed at last
As your hard bat heart gives in.

Love you Batman –
Let's hang around together in your cave
And whisper sweet batnothings –
Oh, I'll love you to the grave.

Love you Batman –
I know Gotham's full of sin,
But maybe you'll visit Bletchley soon
To see your batfan –

Lynne xxx

Stephen Bowkett

The Girl on the Touch Line

Jeanette looked after me when I was little.

Though we are the same age, somehow I was younger.
She taught me soccer skills. When I was old enough
I got selected for our school team, and she didn't.
Simply due to me being a boy, and her being a girl.

She was always more skilful, faster, stronger.
Always more vision, more tactical brain.
So she signed for an all girls' football team
in town. She still gives me lessons, and supports
our school team too. When I score, I look
towards her. Our smiles give us away.
She should be the one picking the ball out of the net.
She doesn't get jealous, mean, angry.
Jeanette has always looked after me.

Philip Burton

Adding It Up

One tomato and one tomato
make two tomatoes
Two bananas and two bananas
make four bananas
Four jellies and four jellies
make eight jellies
Eight feet and eight feet
make sixteen feet
Sixteen feet in heavy boots
stamping on
eight jellies, four bananas and two tomatoes
make
a horrid mess

Dave Calder

Electric Guitars

I like electric guitars:
played mellow or moody
frantic or fast
On CDs or tapes
at home or in cars –
Live, pre-recorded
busked or in bars

I like electric guitars:
played choppy like reggae
or angry like rock
or chirpy like jazz
or strummy like pop
or heavy like metal
it bothers me not

I like electric guitars:
their strings and their straps
and their wild wammy bars
Their jangling and twanging
and funky wah-wahs
Their fuzz boxes, frets
and multi-effects
Pick ups, machine heads
mahogany necks
Their plectrums, their wires
and big amplifiers

I like electric guitars:
played loudly, politely
dully or brightly
daily or nightly
badly or nicely

I like electric guitars:
bass, lead and rhythm –
I basically dig 'em
I like electric guitars

James Carter

Family Album

I wish I liked Aunt Leonora
When she draws in her breath with a hiss
And with fingers of ice and a grip like a vice
She gives me a walloping kiss.

I wish I loved Uncle Nathaniel
(The one with the teeth and the snore).
He's really a pain when he tells me *again*
About what he did in the War.

I really don't care for Aunt Millie,
Her bangles and brooches and beads,
Or the gun that she shoots or those ex-army boots
Or the terrible dogs that she breeds.

I simply can't stand Uncle Albert.
Quite frankly, he fills me with dread
When he gives us a tune with a knife, fork and spoon.
(I don't think he's right in the head.)

I wish I loved Hetty and Harry
(Aunt Hilary's horrible twins)
As they lie in their cots giving off lots and lots
Of gurgles and gargles and grins.

As for nieces or nephews or cousins
There seems nothing else one can do
Except sit in a chair and exchange a cold stare
As if we came out of a zoo.

Though they say blood is thicker than water,
I'm not at all certain it's so.
If you think it's the case, kindly write to this space.
It's something I'm anxious to know.

If we only could choose our relations
How happy, I'm certain, we'd be!
And just one thing more: I am perfectly sure
Mine all feel the same about me.

Charles Causley

First Snow

That day, I woke up early,
and it should have been still dark,
but I sensed a funny sort of glare
that seemed to start beyond the curtains.
There I floated, half asleep,
rubbing my eyes with knuckle-corners
    – until I realized!

Jumped out of bed and shouted, "Snow!"
for everyone to hear me. Dad's deep voice,
all muffled up with blankets, said:
Shut up! Go back to sleep!
    Well, I couldn't.
        Well, you wouldn't!

Goosepimply with the tingly air,
I put on lots of clothes and went downstairs,
quiet as a spider, along the hall,
carrying my wellingtons in my hand,
into the kitchen,
    turned the key slowly, and

Outside. I stood for ages and stared
at a strange new world, where nothing moved.
The roadway had disappeared;
the houses looked like huge igloos, trees
were giant cauliflowers; everything
    stood still.

Nobody else was up, not even the sun,
and the sky was a silver space.
I took a deep breath, and began to run
through the new, white,
    magic place.

When I breathed out, a cloud emerged,
so I nostrilled my dragon-smoke all up the road
with my big leaps, my seven-league boots.
I yelled, and the sound went away
through the grey clear day
    like a shark swimming quickly.

At the end of the lane,
I piled up the snow in a heap that meant
    No Entry.

I snowballed the tin signs over the sweet-shop,
making them clang:
and no one came out to complain.
So I did it again.
Fresh snowflakes were still falling,
    gently.

Later the workmen with shovels
will pile up the day;
lorries with grit will clear the way
for Dad's car trying to start.

There'll be Old Mac the milkman
with his creaky cart
and gloves with long blue fingers;
there'll be shouts in the brilliant air;
there'll be fat white dogs like polar bears
     – later; but now

There's no one but me, the lonely explorer,
up in the dawn where the sun doesn't shine;
breathing and snowballing,
giant-stepping, cat-calling,
hours before breakfast:
     the morning is mine.

                                        Tony Charles

Diwali

Diwali lamps are twinkling, twinkling
In the sky and in our homes and hearts.
We welcome all with cheery greetings
And sweets and patterned *rangoli* art.
Lakshmi flies upon her owl tonight;
Incense curls, our future's sparkling bright.

Debjani Chatterjee

Note: *Rangoli* patterns are drawn at the entrance to
a home to welcome visitors. Lakshmi, the Goddess of
Wealth and Good Fortune, blesses the homes where
lamps are lit in her honour.

Help! Help! Walk For Your Lives!

Astronomers have spotted
The first green trace
Of slime in space.

It comes from a planet
Ten million miles away
Space slugs, the experts say.

It is an invasion
But we on Earth have no need to fear
The slug's top speed is one mile a year.

John Coldwell

How To Be Bad

If you're out on a school trip
and want to be bad,
if you want to drive
your teacher mad.

Don't pull a foul face
or cry out loud,
just shout these words
above a crowd:

"Sir I need the toilet, Sir!
Sir, I fear the worst!
If I don't go now, right away,
I think I'm going to burst."

Then watch as he starts to tremble
watch as he counts to ten,
wait until he gets to eight
then shout those words again.

"Sir I need the toilet, Sir!
Sir, I fear the worst!
If I don't go now, right away,
I think I'm going to burst."

And as people start to pull back
and children move out of line,
get ready to shout again
and scream for one very last time:

"Sir I need the toilet, Sir!
Sir, I fear the worst!
If I don't go now, right away,
I think I'm going to burst."

Then wait until everything falls silent
wait until he spots a loo door,
before smiling and saying politely:
"Sir, I don't want to go any more."

Andrew Collett

The Spearmint Spuggy from Space
Stuck on Every Seat in School

Spuggy on the seat
Chewy on the chair
Bubble gum gunge gets everywhere

It stands on my hands
strands expand like rubber bands.

Congeals and feels like stretch and seal
a scaly skin that you just can't peel.

It smears, here, inside my ears
and round my eyes . . . bubble gum tears.

Beware! It's there
tangled dread locks in my hair.

Look! It's stuck . . .
a pink punk starfish standing up.

It grows all over my nose
so when I breathe a bubble blows

Like polythene or Plasticine
and the bubble that blows is pink and green.

It's pale, a putrid trail
left by a rubber mutant snail
a string vest made from the blubber from a whale
a slimy slug with a six foot tail
syrup stuck on my fingernails.

It clings, like strings
of mouldy maggots and horrible things
on the end of my fingers
a big pink wriggly worm it lingers
so that you cannot distinguish
which is the gum and which are my fingers.

Splashes, splodges, blobs and blots,
blatant blotches, suspect spots,
dabs and dawbs and polka dots
multiplying lots and lots
sticky and strong it has got
the look and feel of alien snot!

Bleargh! Attishyoo!
This alien's trying to kiss you
it's getting to be an issue
one where you wish you
had more than just one Kleenex tissue.

Help! It's drastic
squeezed by snakes of pliable plastic
or an octopus with legs of elastic

Smudges on my shirt
stains on my shoe
a spider's web that's made of glue
I just don't know what to do
with this sticky icky gunged up goo
that pulls so tight my skin turns white
then a nasty ghastly shade of blue.
It's true, I haven't got a clue,
what are we going to do?
It's coming for me and it's coming for you . . .

Invasion of the body snatchers
spuggy on the seats at school will catch us,
plait, matt, attack, attach us.

It's alive, it writhes
chokes your throat and blinds your eyes.

Sticks . . . like sick
thick as an oily slick.

Exploding like a can of worms
that slither and slide and slime and squirm.

Spuggy on the seat
Chewy on the chair
Bubble gum gunge gets everywhere.

So beware! It's here and there!
Bubble gum gunge gets everywhere
and I don't know what to do
it's coming for me and it's coming for you
it's coming for me and it's coming for you
Be careful what you chew
Be careful what you chew
it may just get revenge on you
so be careful
what
you
chew

Paul Cookson

(You Ain't Nothing But A) Hedgehog

You ain't nothing but a hedgehog
Foragin' all the time
You ain't nothing but a hedgehog
Foragin' all the time
You ain't never pricked a predator
You ain't no porcupine.

John Cooper Clarke

Huff

I am in a tremendous huff –
Really, really bad.
It isn't any ordinary huff –
It's one of the best I've had.

I plan to keep it up for a month
Or maybe for a year
And you needn't think you can make me smile
Or talk to you. No fear.

I can do without you and her and them –
Too late to make amends.
I'll think deep thoughts on my own for a while,
Then find some better friends.

And they'll be wise and kind and good
And bright enough to see
That they should behave with proper respect
Towards somebody like me.

I do like being in a huff –
Cold fury is so heady.
I've been like this for half an hour
And it's cheered me up already.

Perhaps I'll give them another chance,
Now I'm feeling stronger,
But they'd better watch out – my next big huff
Could last much, much, much longer.

Wendy Cope

Advice to an Ice Lolly Licker

Red Rocket
on a stick.
If it shines,
lick it quick.

Clap Clap clapclapclap!

Round the edges,
on the top,
round the bottom,
do not stop.

Clap Clap clapclapclap!

Suck the Lolly.
Lick your lips.
Lick the sides
as it drips

Clap Clap clapclapclap!

off the stick –
quick, quick –
lick, lick –
Red Rocket
on a stick.

Clap Clap clapclapclap!

Pie Corbett

Shocked!

Just look at you –
All studs and rings,
Those false nails
And that fake tattoo!
Your hair! My skirt!
Those boots! That hat!
No, Mum, you're NOT
Going out like that!

Sue Cowling

Somewhere!

Somewhere in the halls of wisdom
Lies the largest box.
Filled with all life's little mysteries
And my missing socks!

Ian Deal

Their Secret is Out!

Teachers are not normal.
Anybody knows that –
Only they pretend to be like us
By shopping in the supermarket
And buying jam and cornflakes.
It's a con.
They don't eat.
They are not real inside their bodies –
They are full of wires and micro-circuits.
They feed on mathematics
With spellings like *psoriasis* and *bouillabaisse*
For pud.
Do not believe them when they tell you they were young once.
It is a lie.
The factory that makes them
Does not do "young".
It only makes three sorts:
Bat-eared,
Needle-nosed,
And Eagle-eyed.

Jan Dean

My Sister's Getting Married

My sister's getting married
and it's awful news.
My sister wants a page boy
and it's me she's going to choose!
She's going to buy a satin suit
with frills and lacy stuff,
   a soppy little jacket,
   with soppy little cuffs.

I'm gonna be a page boy!
Please don't tell my mates!
Don't tell 'em where the church is,
Don't tell 'em wedding dates.
   Oh please,
   Oh please don't tell them!

I wish it wasn't true
   My sister's 27
   and I am 42!

Peter Dixon

This Kissing Business

Should I part my lips, or pucker?
Bite them tightly? Blow or suck or

hold my breath? Perhaps I'll practise
on my mirror. See, the fact is

I'm not sure what is expected
when four lips become connected.

Gina Douthwaite

The Shellfish Race

"Are they ready?" asked the flounder, who'd agreed to referee
At the bottom of the Channel just off Angmering On Sea.
"Are you ready?" asked the starter, a pernickety old dab.
"Yes, I'm ready," lisped the lobster. "Yes, I'm ready,"
   croaked the crab.
"Yes, I'm ready," piped the prawn, "although I've got an
   awful limp."
"Yes, I'm ready," called the crawfish. "Yes, I'm ready,"
   squeaked the shrimp.

"On your marks," the starter bubbled: on their marks the
   shellfish got,
Then a flag-like fin was lowered and away the athletes shot
Down a running track so murky and so tangled up with weed
It was difficult to know which one had surged into the lead;
But the lobster beat the crawfish by a short claw to the post
And the sound of fishy cheering echoed up and down the coast.

Third to finish, with a flourish of its feelers, was the shrimp,
Closely followed by the puffed-out prawn, remembering to
   limp;
Then they ran a lap of honour round a boulder in the bay
Before marching off together in a most unshellfish way
To get ready for the revels of the celebration dance –
All except the sideways-scuttling crab who ended up in
   France.

Richard Edwards

Dad's Hiding in the Shed

Dad's hiding in the shed.
He's made me swear
Not to tell Mum
That he's hiding in there.

She was having a lie-down
With the curtains drawn.
We were playing cricket
Out on the lawn.

The scores were level.
It was really tense.
Dad had just hit a six
Right over the fence.

I bowled the next ball
As fast I could.
Dad tried it again
As I knew he would.

But he missed and the ball
Struck him hard on the toe.
He cried out in pain
And, as he did so,

He let go of the bat.
It flew up in an arc
And crashed through the window
Where Mum lay in the dark.

Dad's hiding in the shed.
He's made me swear
Not to tell Mum
That he's hiding in there.

John Foster

Slug

You should feel sorry for the slug –
He has no shell to keep him snug
But slithers round the garden, nude,
Which snails and tortoises think rude.

Hedgehogs, however, think they're swell:
Easy to eat without a shell.

Pam Gidney

Genius

I am a liric maniac
An Urban Oral GENIUS
My style iz fast 'n' FURIOUS
My manna iz SPONTANEOUS
My lirix make yer laugh sometimes
As well as bein SERIOUS
I'll send yer round 'n' round the bend
I'll make yer act DELIRIOUS
Each word is hot, and can't be held
I suppose you'd say I'm DANGEROUS
I know I have a way with wurdz
The wurd I'd use iz NOTORIOUS
For those who want to challenge me
I find it quite RIDICULOUS
When critics try and put me down
Can't see them, they're ANONYMOUS
The only thing I have ter say
I see them all as ODIOUS
I luv my rithmz 'n' the beatz
Smell my wurdz, they're ODOROUS
I love my lirix to the max
Evry syllable 'n' sound iz MARVELLOUS
I execute my wurdz so well
I suppose you'd call it MURDEROUS
To work so hard on all these wurdz
Some say it is LABORIOUS
There's double meaning in my style
Four syllables ter you. AM . . . BIG . . . U . . . OUS
I know I'm going on and on
But I certainly ain't MONOTONOUS

You have ter chill 'n' agree with me
The feeling is UNANIMOUS
Ter get inside yer head like this
I know that I am DEVIOUS
I do it in a sneaky way
I suppose I'd say MISCHIEVOUS
When pepul think about my rimez,
I know that they are CURIOUS
Don't understand the resun why
Becuz the cluez 'R' OBVIOUS
Okay you're right, my wurdz 'R' good
I suppose they are MIRACULOUS
Astounded by this type of rime
I know you 'R' OBLIVIOUS
There'z only one thing left ter say
I'm bad 'n' cool
'N' INFAMOUS

Martin Glynn

Living Doll

My sister was only nine years old
when love first struck her
like a thunderbolt:
six weeks before Christmas
she fell in love . . . with a doll.
A special doll that
– so the adverts claimed –
*"has hair that **really** grows!"*

One flick of the tiny plastic switch and
"so easy"
the neat blonde crop was suddenly
a pony tail.
Another flick and
"in an instant!"
a waist-length mane of golden curls.

She wrote to Father Christmas:
"Please, oh please,
Please – PLEASE!"

She didn't get one.
She got a bike instead –
bought weeks before
and hidden
in the next door neighbours' shed.
She sulked all Christmas.

My mum and dad were sure:
"She'll grow out of it by June"

(her birthday). They were wrong.
This wasn't just another craze.
She kept it up, from January to June,
five months of hints and pleading. Then,
as time grew short, begging letters.
Finally, she left imploring messages
on their Ansaphone.

They gave in,
bought her one, of course.

Her birthday morning;
she tears downstairs,
heart pounding in her throat,
scattering the pile of parcels
on the breakfast table.
There *must* be one.
Is this . . . ?
She skins it – yes!
It is!

A scream of delight and
she runs upstairs
into the bathroom
and locks the door.

Silence.

We sit at breakfast
staring at the untouched presents.

While up above
the silence grows, becomes
suspicious,
unnatural . . .

Then all of a sudden
a scream of real pain –
we leap the stairs three at a time
and there
in the bathroom,
tears streaming down her cheeks,
my sister stands:
the doll in one hand,
my father's razor in the other.

"Grow!" she pleads.
"Please, *please* grow!"

The bald doll grins
its plastic smile unmoved,
while all around my sister's feet
the dreams,
the lovely dreams,
the thick rich golden curls lie

hacked
into
vulgar,
yellow,
nylon
shreds.

                              Mick Gowar

Who Is It?

KLANNNNNG!

tinkletinkletinkletinkle

WoooaaaaH

thumpthumpthumpthump

shuffleshuffleshuffle

eeeeeeeek!

Nobody there.

Gus Grenfell

Nanny Neverley

Old Nanny Neverley
    came from Back There.
She sat in the sunshine
    with frost in her hair.
        I'm going home soon, she said.
        Never said where.

Sweet crumbly biscuits,
    ghostly-grey tea
and a smile would be waiting.
    She listened to me
        and sometimes to someone else
        I couldn't see

and when we fell silent
    and couldn't say why
she glanced at the window.
    She smiled at the sky.
        Look! There, you missed it.
        An angel passed by.

It was one of her stories,
    like: *I'm growing too;*
you grow up, I grow down . . .
    She told lies, I knew.
        Only, now that she's gone
        nothing else seems quite true.

Philip Gross

A Poem Called
"Grown Ups Are Orl Rite If Yoo Eat Them Hot"

That Has Nothing To Do With It

I saw a mouse set cheese traps
One morning after tea,
A fly read the flypaper
And though it seemed strange to me,
A cat burglar was stealing dogs
And right across the street
A lollipop man was being licked
From his head down to his feet.

Mike Harding

There's Very Little Merit in a Ferret

There's very little merit in a ferret
Whipping up your trouser leg
Very little merit in a ferret
Whipping up your trouser leg.

If it were
A pine marten
Oh boy
You'd be smarting
If it were a puma
You'd be dead!

There's very little merit in a ferret
Whipping up your trouser leg,

So if you dote on a stoat
If your heart goes blink for a mink
If you play footloose with a mongoose
If you potter with an otter
If your beazel is a weasel
If your heart is set on a marmoset
Then think

There's very little merit in a ferret
Whipping up your trouser leg.

Ferrets, stoats,
They are vermin
You don't want your underpants
Trimmed with ermine!

There's very little merit in a ferret
Whipping up your trouser leg!

David Harmer

*P.S. When I wrote this poem I made a zoological mistake.
I thought a marmoset was a type of ferret-like creature.
It isn't. It's a small monkey. I meant a marmot . . . which
is, of course, a small type of Bovril.*

Favouritism

When we caught measles
It wasn't fair –
My brother collected
Twice his share.

He counted my spots:
"One hundred and twenty!"
Which sounded to me
As if I had plenty.

Then I counted his –
And what do you think?
He'd two hundred and thirty-eight,
Small, round and pink!

I felt I'd been cheated
So "Count mine again!"
I told him, and scowled
So he dared not complain.

"One hundred and twenty" –
The same as before . . .
In our house, he's youngest
And he always gets more!

Trevor Harvey

The Emergensea

The octopus awoke one morning and wondered what
   rhyme it was.
Looking at his alarm-clocktopus
he saw that it had stopped
and it was time to stop having a rest
and get himself dressed.
On every octofoot
he put
an octosocktopus
but in his hurry, one foot got put
not into an octosock
but into an electric plug socket
and the octopus got a nasty electric shocktopus
and had to call the octodoctopus
who couldn't get in
to give any help or medicine
because the door was loctopus.
The octopus couldn't move, being in a state of
   octoshocktopus
so the octodoctopus bashed the door
to the floor
and the cure was a simple as could be:
a nice refreshing cup of seawater.

John Hegley

49

No Trespassers

Do not explore on Rannoch Moor*
as dark descends and spectres roar,
when peat bogs boil and you're alone,
where puking spooks garrotte and groan.

There's shapes that scream on Rannoch Moor,
broad shadow beasts which gouge and gore.
There's bats and rats to drink your veins
and gangly ghouls that swallow trains.

Ogres og on Rannoch Moor –
they must have someone fresh to gnaw,
and owls chew eyes and spiders crush
each human being to slurp-size mush.

So tremble, fret and be unsure
if you should stray on Rannoch Moor.
Best stay off if you guard your health . . .
. . . I must keep Rannoch to myself.

Stewart Henderson

* Rannoch Moor: a beautiful, mainly uninhabited
wilderness in the Scottish Highlands.

Cake-Face

I like chocolate
cake, I like birthday
cake, I like ginger
cake, I like sponge
cake, I like fruit
cake, I like Christmas
cake, I like carrot
cake, I just can't stand
      stoma
cake.

David Horner

All Change!

All Change! All Change!

When the guard on the train
or when the bus driver
shouts "All change!"
and everyone has to
grab their things
in a grumbling fluster
and get out again –

just suppose
it was a magician
in disguise
playing a trick,
and in two ticks
all
the shoppers and schoolkids,
mums and dads,
with their papers and cases
and carrier bags,
grandpas, grans,
football fans,
and tourists with their maps
and their tired feet
did change –

and found themselves
out in the street
like a runaway zoo,
with
a bear or two,
a caribou
and a worm, perhaps –
tigers and mice,
a wasp,
a frog,
aardvarks,
ducks
and a kangaroo-dog,
a crocodile,
a chimpanzee –
and a few left behind on board,
a sunflower,
a couple of stones
and a
tree –

What do you think you'd be?

Libby Houston

The Rhyming Bat

Ian McMillan
was a poet
whose poems
occasionally rhymed.
Sometimes they did
and sometimes they didn't
and nobody seemed to care.

Sometimes his poems
were free as sweet papers
Blowing in the breeze

and they were sometimes as noisy
as wallpaper scrapers
scratching the leaves
off the Autumn trees . . .

But
Ian McMillan
was a poet
whose poems
occasionally rhymed.
Sometimes they did
and sometimes they didn't
and nobody seemed to bother.

And then he got bitten
By the Rhyming Bat
that flies through the forest at night
and rhyme began
to seep into his poems
before the morning light . . .

Because the Rhyming Bat
is a Deadly Bat
whose bite leaves you desperate for rhyme
and you rhyme all the time
and you rhyme and you rhyme
and your poems go on rhyming all day
and the rhymes won't stop coming
like some incessant drumming
and the rhyming is rhyming to stay.

Ian McMillan
was a poet
whose poems occasionally rhymed.
Sometimes they did
and sometimes they didn't
and nobody seemed to mind

nobody seemed to mind . . .

Nobody seemed to mind . . .

MORAL:

Try not to get bitten
by the Rhyming Bat
or that will be
the end of that.

Ian McMillan

Something to Say

Pigeons "Coo" and parrots shriek.
Cats "Miaow" when mice squeak, "Eek!"
Llamas spit! Snakes hissssss snakecharmers.
I've never spoken to piranhas;
but when chimpanzees hoot, "Oo oo oo,"
I say, "Pleased to meet you."

Skunks yell "Keep away!" with stinks.
An octopus can squirt black ink.
Termite troupes chit-chat all day.
Giraffes laugh, if zebras bray;
but when chimpanzees hoot, "Oo oo oo,"
I say, "Pleased to meet you."

Gorilla chaps shout, "Slap, slap, slap."
Electric eels can zap, zap, zap.
Frogs makes jokes, "Croak, croak, croak, croak."
When my dog met a hog, er, neither spoke;
but when chimpanzees hoot, "Oo oo oo,"
I say, "Pleased to meet you."

Ink or stink, slap, zap or shriek;
"Baaa", "Woof", "Moo", "Oink", "Croak" and "Eek!"
Species, in their special way,
have something that they want to say.
But when chimpanzees hoot, "Oo oo oo,"
I say, "Pleased to meet you."

Mike Johnson

Towards the End of Summer

Cherry red and honey bee
Buzzed around the summer flowers
Bumbled round the luscious fruits.
Patient weaver clambered by.

Silently while the others bobbed
And busied in the bright blue air
Hither, zither, merrily,
Weaver waved his cool brown arms
And gently drew around the tree
Silken skeins so fine so fine
No one could see that they were there,
Until one Autumn morning when
Cherry was gone and bee asleep
A silver shawl was laced across the grass
With little beads like pearls strung all along.

Jenny Joseph

Temper Temper

He kicked it, he smacked it,
He got a stick and whacked it;
But no matter how much he attacked it,
He couldn't make it move.

He pulled at it, he tore at it,
He shouted and he swore at it;
But no matter how much he got sore at it,
He couldn't make it move.

So Dad left his car at the shops,
caught a bus home,
and was cross with us for the rest of the day.

Mike Jubb

Word of a Lie

I am the fastest runner in my school and that's
NO WORD OF A LIE
I've got gold fillings in my teeth and that's
NO WORD OF A LIE
In my garden, I've got my own big bull and that's
NO WORD OF A LIE
I'm brilliant at giving my enemies grief and that's
NO WORD OF A LIE
I can multiply three billion and twenty-seven by nine billion
   four thousand and one in two seconds and that's
NO WORD OF A LIE
I can calculate the distance between planets before you've
   had toast and that's
NO WORD OF A LIE
I can always tell when my best pals boast and that's
NO WORD OF A LIE
I'd been round the world twice before I was three and a
   quarter and that's
NO WORD OF A LIE
I am definitely my mother's favourite daughter and that's
NO WORD OF A LIE
I am brilliant at fake laughter. I go Ha aha Ha ha ha and
   that's
NO WORD OF A LIE
I can tell the weather from one look at the sky and that's
NO WORD OF A LIE
I can predict disasters, floods, earthquakes and murders
   and that's
NO WORD OF A LIE

I can always tell when other people lie and that's
NO WORD OF A LIE
I can even tell if someone is going to die and that's
NO WORD OF A LIE
I am the most popular girl in my entire school and that's
NO WORD OF A LIE
I know the golden rule, don't play the fool, don't boast, be
    shy and that's
NO WORD OF A LIE
I am sensitive, I listen, I have kind brown eyes and that's
NO WORD OF A LIE

You don't believe me do you?
ALL RIGHT, ALL RIGHT, ALL RIGHT
I am the biggest liar in my school and that's
NO WORD OF A LIE

Jackie Kay

Tree and Leaf

Said the tree to the leaf –
    Move over!
It's time for you
    to go.
There's winter round
    the corner
and somebody spoke
    of snow.
Under the frost's
    cold finger
my buds are growing
    fat.
The fires of spring
    are smouldering –
what do you think
    of that?

Said the leaf to the tree –
    I'm going!
It's time for me
    to fall . . .
I'm frail, and thin,
    and trembly . . .
I burn, like a golden
    ball.
I sing, with my silent
    beauty,
I float
    among streams of air,
and the living earth
    receives me
when oak and beech
    are bare.

Jean Kenward

Are You There?

Are you cold?
Did you shiver?
Did you see the curtain quiver?

Did you hear it?
Softly speaking
Did you hear the staircase creaking?

Can you smell it?
Sweet and sickly
Does your hair feel wet and prickly?

Can you see it?
Through the gloom?
Is it with us in the room?

Are you listening?
Can you hear me?
Can you?

Craig King

Lips

There are greasy lips and sleazy lips,
Easy lips and cheesy lips,
The kind that make you queasy lips.
There are winter-cold and sneezy lips
And far too bright and breezy lips.
Some frighten you with freezy lips
Or shrink you with lean, mean, teasy lips.

Some like lips that speak sharp and crisp.
I prefer those lips with a gentle lisp!

John Kitching

When Mum Finally Went to Pieces

When Mum finally
went to pieces

I found bits
of her all over
the house.

She left
one leg
in the bathroom

the other
in the hall.

One arm
was in
the kitchen

whilst the other
was hanging around
in the attic.

The rest of her
turned up in
various places
throughout the house.

Eventually
I found her head
taking a short nap
on the sofa
in the living-room

so I asked her
if there was anything
I could do
to help?

But she told me
not to worry
and said

she'd soon
pull herself

together.

Tony Langham

Stock Cupboard Rap

In our teacher's stock cupboard
With his paper and pens,
Lurk all sorts
Of his peculiar friends.

Large and small, fat and thin,
You'd better watch out if you need to go in!

There's a little brown hairy one
That lives on the floor,
And will bite your leg
When you come through the door!

Large and small, fat and thin,
You'd better watch out if you need to go in!

The long thin furry one
Sits on the shelf,
Show him a mirror
And he'd frighten himself!

Large and small, fat and thin,
You'd better watch out if you need to go in!

The teeny black fuzzy one
Hides among the pens,
With fangs like that
He hasn't many friends!

Large and small, fat and thin,
You'd better watch out if you need to go in!

But the hairiest, scariest creature of all
Clings like a limpet up on the wall.
When you creep inside he stretches his limbs,
And tickles your head, among other things!

Large and small, fat and thin,
You'd better watch out if you need to go in!

So take great care if you have to find
A pencil, a rubber or a pen of some kind.
To go in that cupboard takes nerves of steel,
Cos if one doesn't get you –
ANOTHER ONE WILL!!

Anne Logan

If You Were Made of Chocolate

If you were made of chocolate
    would you eat yourself?
Or be dressed in silver paper
    on the sweetshop shelf?

Would you have a crunchy middle
    or be filled with fudge toffee?
Would you have a special offer price
    give ten per cent more free?

Would you be long and thin and flaky
    or chunky in a bar
or sweet and sticky pieces
    filling up a jar?

If you were made of chocolate
    would you be nibbled bit by bit
or stuffed into a mouth in one huge go?
    (Your mum would have a fit!)

If you were made of chocolate
    you'd have to mind the sun
and if your friends got hungry, well –
    it wouldn't be much fun!

If you were made of chocolate
    would you eat yourself?
Or would you sit for ever
    on life's dusty sweetshop shelf?

Rupert Loydell

The Phantom's Fang-tastic Show

The Phantom says,
"Roll up! Roll up for Spectres!
Roll up for Apparitions!
Come in and see the Gremlins
– all sizes, shapes, conditions.
To see my Show to best effect
put on these weirdo 3D specs
From 'Spec-ter-al Opticians'!"

The Phantom says,
"Roll up! Roll up for Werewolves!
See dopey Doppelgängers!
Come in and watch my Hellcats
mud-wrestling with Headbangers!
In order to protect your lugs
make sure you wear these ear-hole plugs
when Draculas drop clangers!"

The Phantom says,
"Roll up! Roll up for Ghosties!
See Demons disembowelling!
You must not miss the Mummy
seal-wrapped in ancient towelling!
You'll need to don this steel-lined hat
as things go Whizz! Crash! Wallop! Splat!
when Poltergeists are prowling!"

The Phantom says,
"Roll up! Roll up for Zombies!
Watch nifty Necromancers!
My wacky whistling Wizards
are fabulous entrancers!
You'll nod your head and tap your feet
to spooky band – 'The Banshee Beat'.
You'll *love* the UnDead-Dancers!"

"So,
Roll up for my Fang-tastic Show!
Be quick, we're starting in a mo.
Come in and view a creepy cast.
The last few seats are filling fast.
Make haste!
There is no time to spare.
Please take your places
. . . if you dare!"

Wes Magee

Close-Cropped Hair

Close-cropped hair feels good.
It should.
It gives you street cred –
And, as I've always said,
It feels like having eyebrows
All over your head.

Linda Marshall

Ice-Cream Poem

The chiefest of young Ethel's vices
Was eating multitudes of ices.

Whene'er the ice-van's booming tinkle
Was heard, Eth ran out in a twinkle,

And gorged herself on large 'Vanilla';
Her mum foretold that it would kill 'er

No tears could thaw her; once she ran
Away and hid inside the van,

And promptly froze upon the spot
Like the saltpillar-wife of Lot.

Poor Eth is licked! Behold the follies
Of one whose lolly went on lollies.

Though there is one thing in her favour
She now has quite a strawberry flavour.

Gerda Mayer

It is always the same dream...

He's with them,
Driving late at night,
Alone.

Very tired.

Very lost.

There's a light
Above the treetops
Singing

Red
And
Yellow
And
Pink
And
Green

Any colour
You'd care
To imagine.

The engine fades.

Headlights die.

And they're two hours
Down the road.

Five miles missing.

Kevin McCann

Potato Clock

A potato clock, a potato clock
    Has anybody got a potato clock?
A potato clock, a potato clock
    Oh where can I find a potato clock?

I went down to London the other day
Found myself a job with a lot of pay
Carrying bricks on a building site
From early in the morning till late at night

No one here works as hard as me
I never even break for a cup of tea
My only weakness, my only crime
Is that I can never get to work on time

A potato clock, a potato clock
    Has anybody got a potato clock?
A potato clock, a potato clock
    Oh where can I find a potato clock?

I arrived this morning half an hour late
The foreman came up in a terrible state
"You've got a good job, but you'll lose it, cock,
If you don't get up at eight o'clock."

Up at eight o'clock, up at eight o'clock
    Has anybody got up at eight o'clock?
Up at eight o'clock, up at eight o'clock
    Oh where can I find up at eight o'clock?

Roger McGough

Song of the Homeworkers

Homework, moanwork
Cross it out and groanwork

Homework, neat work
Keeps you off the street work

Homework, moanwork
Cross it out and groanwork

Homework, roughwork
When you've had enough work

Homework, moanwork
Cross it out and groanwork

Homework, dronework
Do it on your own work

Homework, moanwork
Cross it out and groanwork

Homework, gloomwork
Gaze around the room work

Homework, moanwork
Cross it out and groanwork

Homework, guesswork
Book is in a mess work

Homework, moanwork
Cross it out and groanwork

Homework, rushwork
Do it on the bus work

Homework, moanwork
Cross it out and groanwork

Homework, hatework
Hand your book in late work

Homework, moanwork
Cross it out and groan g r o a n GROANWORK!

Trevor Millum

Ode to my Nose

O Nose
Why perch upon my Face?
Could you not find
A better place?

You jut between
One Eye and tother
So neither Eye
Can see his Brother.

An easy target
For the hostile Fist.
You're an obstruction
When I want to be kissed.

And when you run
It's always South
Over my top lip
Into my Mouth.

O Nose
Why perch upon my Face?
Could you discover
No better place?

My Nose replied:
Up here I have come
As far as possible
From your Bum.

Adrian Mitchell

Make a Face

I can make a fat face,
a dog face, a cat face.
I can make a thin face,
a skinny little pin face.
I can make a mad face,
a horrid, mean and bad face,
a sick face, a sad face,
a rather like my dad face.
I can make a funny face,
a just as sweet as honey face.
I can make a happy face,
a sharp snarl and snappy face.
I can make a true face,
a just for me and you face.
But this face,
you ain't seen this face –
NO PLACE!

Tony Mitton

The Invisible Man

The invisible man is a joker
Who wears an invisible grin
And the usual kind of visible clothes
Which cover up most of him,

But there's nothing above his collar
Or at the end of his sleeves,
And his laughter is like the invisible wind
Which rustles the visible leaves.

When the visible storm clouds gather
He strides through the visible rain
In a special invisible see-through cloak
Then invisibly back again.

But he wears a thick, visible overcoat
To go out when it visibly snows
And the usual visible footprints
Get left wherever he goes.

In the visible heat-haze of summer
And the glare of the visible sun,
He undoes his visible buttons
With invisible fingers and thumb,

Takes off his visible jacket,
Loosens his visible tie,
Then snaps his visible braces
As he winks an invisible eye.

Last thing in his visible nightgown
Tucked up in his visible bed
He rests on a visible pillow
His weary invisible head

And ponders by visible moonlight
What invisibility means
Then drifts into silent invisible sleep
Full of wonderful visible dreams.

                                        John Mole

United Together

I've got two legs,
Two arms, one nose,

Two ears, two eyes,
Ten fingers, ten toes,

One back, one brain,
One bum, one belly,

Two lips, two hands,
Two feet (they're smelly!)

One heart, one head,
One voice, one face,

And united together,
I'm the human race.

Darren Moody

Limerick

There was a young fellow called Wood
Whose limericks weren't very good
All would go fine
Till he reached the last line
When for some inexplicable reason . . . but possibly as a
result of falling from his pram when only six months old
and receiving a nasty blow on the head after which his
behaviour was always somewhat eccentric and caused a
considerable amount of embarrassment to his parents
brothers sisters grandparents aunts uncles cousins great-
aunts great-uncles cousins once removed cousins twice
removed and most of his friends . . . he tried to cram in as
many words as he possibly could.

Marcus Moore

A to Z

A up said me dad,
B off to bed with you.
C it's half past eight and I've
Decided that from now on it's bed before nine.
E can't be serious I thought.
F he carries on like this I'll never see any TV
G I'll lose my grasp of American slang.
H not fair.
I won't go.
J think I should protest?
K I will.
L o said me dad,
M not standing for this
N y kid thinks he can disobey me has got another think
    coming.
O yes he has!
P, then wash your hands and face, do your teeth and
    straight to bed.
Q then, your sisters will have finished soon.
R you ready yet? Wash that face properly
S pecially round your nose. It's disgusting.
T? No you can't. If you drink tea now you will wet the bed
U will you know.
V end of a perfect day. Now I'll tuck you in
W up to save space. Then I can fit your brother in too –
    and the dog and hamster. There you all fit in
Xactly
Y don't you like it? It's cosy, space-saving, economical.
    Go to sleep. Not a peep Do exactly as I
ZZZZZZZZZZZZZZZzz.

Michaela Morgan

84

Bigfoot

Our house is full of Bigfoot
or should that be Bigfeet?
We watched them from our window
as they stumbled down the street.

They knocked upon our door
and asked to come inside.
"Don't leave us here," they pleaded,
"We need a place to hide."

Now there's Bigfeet in the kitchen
and Biggerfeet in the hall.
On a patch of grass in our garden,
Bigfeet are playing football.

There's Bigfeet in our garage
and Bigfeet in the shed,
while underneath the duvet,
Bigfeet sleep in my bed.

Bigfeet lounge in the lounge
all watching our TV.
There's nowhere much to sit
since they've broken our settee.

Some Bigfoot put his foot
right through our bedroom ceiling.
The darkness in our loft, he said,
was really quite appealing.

The airing cupboard Bigfoot
keeps our water hot.
"No problem at all," he says,
"I like this job a lot."

They make an awful racket
up and down our stairs,
they queue to use the bathroom
and block the sink with hairs.

At night they growl and snore,
loud as a thunderstorm,
but all these fur coats everywhere
Keep us cosy and warm!

Brian Moses

Have You Read...?

Enjoy your Homework by R.U. Joking
Out for the Count by I.C. Stars
Cliff-Top Rescue by Justin Time
A Year in Space by Esau Mars

Your Turn to Wash Up by Y. Mee
Off to the Dentist by U. First
Broken Windows by E. Dunnett
Pickpocket Pete by M.T. Purse

Lions on the Loose by Luke Out
Helping Gran by B.A. Dear
Ten Ice Creams by Segovia Flaw
Rock Concert by Q. Here

Judith Nicholls

The Glaisdale Schoolyard Alliance of 1974

At school
Valerie, Debby and Netta
were the best of friends

but
you'd never see all three of them together
only ever two at a time
always having fell out with the third
Val and Debby together
then Val and Netta
then Debby and Netta

At school
Valerie, Debby and Netta
were the best of friends
they all hated Sandra Vickers

Henry Normal

Mr Kipling

When I'm feeling like a snack,
I like doughnuts and flapjack,
Angel cake or gingerbread or Bakewell tart;
But when it's time for lunch
It's Battenburg or almond crunch,
A dozen madeleines is just the start;
I'll polish off a flan
With chopped nuts and marzipan,
Then I'm on to cake, both cherry and Dundee;
I'll munch my way through oodles
Of iced buns and apple strudels,
And save the macaroons and petits fours for tea!

And it's cake, cake! cake!
There's no other food to beat it,
So let the peasants eat it,
There's nothing so delicious as a cake!

If I'm ready for a blow-out
I'll put on my coat and go out
To Tesco and inspect their stock of cake;
If I find some walnut squares,
Forest gateaux or eclairs,
Just waiting on the shelves for me to take;
If I see an almond slice,
Or Swiss roll, I'll say "How nice",
And buy 'em with a piece of fruit Madeira,
And when my plate of cake's diminished,
I'm not sad that lunch has finished . . .
Because it means that tea is getting nearer!

And it's cake, cake! cake!
There's no other food to beat it,
So let the peasants eat it,
There's nothing so delicious as a cake!

David Orme

The Tent by the Sea

I know an old woman called Mary McHutch
Who lives in a tent by the sea
Where she keeps a black box
Which she never unlocks,
And she's buried the old iron key.
She's buried the old iron key in the sand
And deep in the damp dark it lies,
Whilst she taps and she knocks
On the old iron box
As she murmurs and mutters and sighs.

Oh, what have you got in your old iron box
In your tent by the sea, Miss McHutch?
Is it rubies and pearls, silk gowns for young girls,
Lockets and earrings and such?
Lockets and earrings and rubies and pearls
And birds made of gold in a tree?
Is it these that you keep
In the dark while you sleep,
Near the box in the tent by the sea?

In the box, in the tent, said Mary McHutch,
There are things that are not meant for show.
They stay unrevealed
When lips have been sealed –
There are secrets which no one must know.
There are secrets which no one must know, little friend,
And I've buried the old iron key,
The key that unlocks
My black, iron box
In the dark, in the tent, by the sea.

Jack Ousbey

Bully

Pick me out straight off
Yeah that's me
See?
There by the steps
See?
Bigger than the rest
Stronger too
Know what I mean
Best fighter in school me.
You watch 'em
Watch 'em when they line up
Nobody catches my eye
Nobody
Too scared see.
Try it on with me
See what they'll get;
Knee in the leg
Arm up the back see
Like that
Know what I mean
Like that!
They daren't tell nobody
Not the headteacher
Not their mums and dads
They know what they'll get.

Yeah they know.
So just watch out
Yeah you
Talkin' to you.
Keep it shut
Or else
Know what I mean
Unless you want that
And more of that
Understand?
Understand?
You'd better.

Gareth Owen

The Pet Habit

I'm fed up people telling me
I've got a nasty habit.
But I have. It's true. I do.

I keep it in a box full of dirty straw.
I feed it nose-pickings and belches,
Bits of spit and bum-scratches.
It's a nasty little habit.
When people ask, "What's in the box?"
I say, "It's my pet habit."
"Don't you mean pet rabbit?" they ask.
"No," I say, and show them.
"That's a nasty little habit," they say.

Brian Patten

The Moon is on the Microphone
(A Country Rap)

Oh the trees are dressing for an all night bop
And the sheep are going bonkers as they do the Heron Hop,
And the little leaf sister
How she boogies with the breeze
As the cows do the rhythm
With the spoons on their knees.
All the birds are singin'
On the Top of the Plops!
And the wind he is drumming
With a bunch of carrot tops.
The sheep are looking chic
In the latest woolly style,
As they hop a happy conga
In a crocodile file;
And the stars are driven down
From their mansions in the sky,
The clouds would like a dance
But they dare not even try,
So they cry-baby, hey-baby, grumble and sigh!

And the Moon is on the microphone,
Crooning quite a tune
As every blade of grass
Is falling to a swoon.
Wow!
What a bop
'Til you drop
In a bucket of slop,
What a sight,
What a night,
What an animal rite!

Andrew Fusek Peters

Mrs Thirkettle

Stiff as bristles on an old yard broom

There are –

Black as lonely midnight shadows

three hairs –

Long as a fisherman's lying fish

in the wart –

Thick as gravy left over from Sunday

on the cheek –

Bigger than the trees in the park

of Mrs Thirkettle.

Can you go to the office,
says the teacher

– she knows.

And fetch some blue chalk?
says the teacher

– she's afraid.

Oh and can you get the register too?
says the teacher

– she knows the fear.

Iwillnotthink . . .   . . . !
Iwillnotthink . . .   . . . !
Iwillnotthink . . .   . . . !

(I will not think about the wart!)

too late –

Far too late.

I knock and march in

(Hairy wart)

I knock and march straight in

(Ugly hairy wart)

I will not think about the – shhh! nearly!

(Massive, big, ugly, hairy wart)

I knock and march in

(My heart in my socks)

I knock and march right in

(Pounding fear, awful panic)

I knock and march in

(I've never seen her eyes!)

I knock and march straight in

(never seen her lips!)

I knock and march in

(never seen her nose!)

I knock, march in,
   and look her straight
    in the wart.

I.R. Eric Petrie

Interrogation in the Nursery

Infant: What's that?
Inspector: What?
Infant: That on your face.
Inspector: It's a moustache.
Infant: What does it do?
Inspector: It doesn't do anything.
Infant: Oh.
Inspector: It just sits there on my lip.
Infant: Does it go up your nose?
Inspector: No.
Infant: Could I stroke it?
Inspector: No.
Infant: Is it alive?
Inspector: No, it's not alive.
Infant: Can I have one?
Inspector: No, little girls don't have moustaches.
Infant: Why?
Inspector: Well, they just don't.
Infant: Can I have one when I grow up?
Inspector: No, ladies don't have moustaches either.
Infant: Well my granny's got one!

Gervase Phinn

The Klorine Kid

They call me the Klorine Kid,
I go swimming every day.
They call me the Klorine Kid,
I'm the King of the Baths, OK?

Make a splash
Make waves
Belly up
Not afraid
Roll over
Belly down
Never scared
Of going down

Deep end
Shallow end
Catch my breath
Not the bends
Try a dive
From the top
Watch out for
The belly flop

Doggy paddle
Woof! Woof!
Butterfly
Flap! Flap!
Do the backstroke
Really slow
Quick! The crawl!
Watch me go!

Treading water
Gulping air
Water water
Everywhere
Wet skin
Shake dry
Where's my towel?
Must fly

They call me the Klorine Kid,
I go swimming every day.
They call me the Klorine Kid,
I'm the King of the Baths, OK?

Simon Pitt

But Of Course There Was Nobody There!

Just when I thought they'd all gone
and I'd sat down to read a good book,
there was a loud creak on the landing
and I dashed up to take a look.

But of course there was nobody there.

Settled once more in my chair
reading a poem about a twin lamb,
I nearly jumped out of my skin
when I heard the kitchen door slam.

But of course there was nobody there!

There came a sort of a groan
from the back of the house somewhere.
Then shocked by the shrill of the phone
I picked it up and answered with care.

But of course there was nobody there.

My nerves were now torn to shreds.
My heart was beating much faster.
I wished I was not on my own –
the day was a total disaster.

But of course there was nobody there.

Now frightened and ready to scream
I buried my head in my arms,
only to be roused from my terror
when the door bell rang like an alarm.

Would there be somebody there?

Scared and dripping with sweat
I went and opened the door.
Outside on the step lay a card
saying "I rang till my finger was sore –

But there seemed to be no one there."

I looked at myself in a mirror
And was startled by what I saw
There was absolutely no sign of me
I checked the mirror once more,

But I definitely wasn't there!

Janis Priestley

Break-Time Phrase Book

Givuzacrisp!
May I please share your snack?

Gerroffmeefut!
Would you kindly move your weight from my toes?

Wodyameenitzafoul?
Are you suggesting that my football technique does not
   comply with the rules?

Stopshuvvin!
Please do not invade my personal space.

Awlerruzavanutherminnitmiz!
Dear teacher, would you kindly allow us a little longer?

Gerrinkwikorwivadit!
Our teacher will not be very pleased if we're late.

(You can make a phrase book for dinner time)

Rita Ray

Seaside Song

It was a
sun-boiled, bright light, fried egg, hot skin, sun-tanned
sssizzzzzzler of a day.

It was a
pop song, ding-dong, candy floss, dodgem car, arcade, no
shade
smashing seaside town.

We had
a well time, a swell time, a real pell-mell time,
a fine time, a rhyme time, a super double-dime time.

We
beach swam, ate ham, gobbled up a chicken leg,
climbed trees, chased bees,
got stuck in sand up to our knees,
played chase, flew in space,
beat a seagull in a skating race,
rowed boats, quenched throats,
spent a load of £5 notes,
sang songs, hummed tunes,
played hide and seek in sandy dunes.

Did all these things
too much by far
that we fell asleep going back in the car
from the seaside.

John Rice

When my Dad Watches the News

When my dad watches the news . . .
You can start lots of fights
And swing from the lights,
You can throw all the cushions about,
You can smash every plate,
Keep on slamming the gate
And wear all your clothes inside out;
Do a dangerous trick
Or make yourself sick
By eating four packets of jelly,
You can "prune" a few plants,
Donated by aunts,
Or draw Superman on his belly;
You can dig up the garden
Burp, and not say pardon,
Or write on the wall with a pen,
You can shout, "There's a fire!"
Or, "Mum's joined a choir!"
Or, "I'm leaving school when I'm ten!"
You can dance on the table,
For as long as you're able,
Then dive off the edge with real "flare",
You can hair-gel the cat
So she's painful to pat,
You can staple your gran to the chair;
Phone a friend, in New York,
And have a long talk,
Or tell him, "You've won a world cruise."

You can juggle with eggs
Or shave the dog's legs,
When my dad watches the news.

Coral Rumble

Secret Affair

our love is like
a red, red
nose
embarrassing
and somehow
conspicuous

let's hope
we don't
blow it

Andrew Rumsey

Gecko

The goggle eyed gecko

Stealthily goes

Creeping along

On his velcroed toes,

Flicking his tongue

To catch the flies,

Gecko, gecko

Goggle eyes.

Anita Marie Sackett

My Dog

My dog belongs to no known breed,
A bit of this and that.
His head looks like a small haystack
He's lazy, smelly, fat.

If I say, "Sit!", he walks away.
When I throw stick or ball
He flops down in the grass as if
He had no legs at all,

And looks at me with eyes that say,
"You threw the thing, not me.
You want it back, then get it back.
Fair's fair, you must agree."

He is a thief. Last week but one
He stole the Sunday Roast
And showed no guilt at all as we
Sat down to beans on toast.

The only time I saw him run –
And he went like a flash –
Was when a mugger in the park
Tried to steal my cash.

My loyal brave companion flew
Like a missile to the gate
And didn't stop till safely home.
He left me to my fate.

And would I swap him for a dog
Obedient, clean and good,
An honest, faithful, lively chap?
Oh boy, I would! I would!

Vernon Scannell

Auntie's Boyfriend

Auntie's brought her boyfriend home. He's sitting in a chair.
He wears an earring and he's got no hair.

He's crazy about football and I'm glad about that.
He's polite to my granny, he's kind to the cat
But I have to make an effort not to stand and stare
Cos he wears an earring and he's got no hair.

He eats his dinner nicely. His manners are OK.
He sips his tea in silence in an ordinary way.
He nibbles with decorum at a chocolate eclair –
But he wears an earring and he's got no hair.

I'll ring up the gang, I'll ring them for a dare:
"Come round this evening, there's a secret I must share.
My auntie's brought her boyfriend home. He's sitting in a chair
And he wears an earring and he's got no hair."

Fred Sedgwick

How To Successfully Persuade Your Parents To Give You More Pocket Money

Ask, request, demand, suggest, cajole or charm
Ingratiate, suck up to, flatter, compliment or smarm
Negotiate, debate, discuss, persuade, convince, explain
Or reason, justify, protest, object, dispute, complain
Propose, entreat, beseech, beg, plead, appeal, implore
Harass, go on about it, pester, whinge, whine, nag and bore
Annoy, insult, reproach, denounce, squeal, scream and shout
Go quiet, subdued, look worried, fret, brood, tremble,
    shiver, pout
Act depressed, downhearted, upset, snivel, sigh
Go all glum and plaintive, wobble bottom lip and cry
Sniff, sulk, grumble, stare at ceiling, mope, pine, stay in bed
Get cross, get angry, fume, seethe, fester, agitate, see red
Provoke, enrage, push, bully, aggravate and goad
Screech, smoke, burn up, ignite, spark, detonate,
    EXPLODE

And if all that doesn't work

Here are two little tricks
That should do it with ease

No 1: smile
No 2: say please

                                        Andrea Shavick

When I Grow Up

I want to be:

A systems analyst,
A game-show panellist,
A pop star
With a guitar,
A technologist,
A psychologist,
A herpetologist,

A man who studies volcanoes
An ecologist?
No, a seismologist!

I want to be:

Something in the city,
Very pretty,
A fortune teller
A good speller,

A radar technician,
Always out fishin',
A clever magician,
A cosmetician,
A politician,

A dress designer,
A coal miner,
A good rhymer,
A charmer,
A pig farmer,

A rock and roller,
A South Pole explorer,
A moonwalker,
A New Yorker;

I want to be:

Stinking rich,
A wicked witch,
A private eye,
An engineer,
A life peer,

A DJ
OK?
A lead singer,
A right winger
For Liverpool,
Cool!

I want to be:

Taller,
Thinner,
A lottery winner!

But if none
Of these can be
I will remain
Yours truly
ME!

Matt Simpson

999!

"Nine . . . nine . . . er . . . NINE!
Er, hello, is that the emergency . . . thingy . . . services?
It is! Oh good!
Well I've got a little bit of a problem.
You see . . .
My name?
Mark.
No – MARK – as in SPARK
which is – er – part of my problem, you see.
What's happened?
Well I was sort of making
this birthday cake for my cat.
Yeah – that's right my CAT!
Why, have you got one?
No honest, this is an emergency.
Yeah I will try to be quick
but I need to tell you so you know, right!
Now my cat likes birthday cake,
especially licking the icing sugar,
and it was . . .
that's right his birthday!
Yes I will hurry.
Anyway I sort of splodged everything together
BUT . . . the butter was a bit hard
So I put it in a pan to sort of soften it up
and you'll be glad to hear that it did!
Trouble is I – er – kinda forgot about it
and I've sort of – er – set the house on fire!
So do you think you could send round one of those
nice, noisy, red fire engines

and tell them to bring plenty of water.
Oh and – er – an ambulance.
Well my mum and dad are a little bit . . . er . . . unconscious.
Oh and I suppose – er – the police.
Well, when my mum and dad sort of wake up
I think they're going to be a bit cross and murder me!
Where do I live?
In this street, next to the corner shop
which serves my favourite ice cream.
Anyway I'd better go now because
it is getting rather warm in here
and I haven't found the cat yet.
Bye-Dee-Bye!"

Ian Souter

Treasure Trail

Normally
I get home from school
and go straight out again
to the park
but today

I spotted a penny on the hall floor
and as I bent to pick it up
I spotted another –
one pace away

As I bent to pick that up
I spotted another –
one pace away

As I bent to pick that up
I spotted yet another
on the bottom step
of the stairs

I picked it up
and spied another
on the third step

and another on the seventh
and another on the tenth
and another at the top

At the top of the stairs
I spotted a five p
on the landing –
one pace away

At this rate I was going to be rich.
I followed the trail
to the door of my room

The door was open
and I could see
a ten p
on my floor

I went in and,
as I bent to pick it up,
the door slammed shut
behind me.

I tried to open it
but it was shut fast.
A note was pinned to the door

It said, You are my prisoner!
You are not getting out
until you have tidied your room!
Signed
Mum

And all for
twenty-five p!

Roger Stevens

In the Desert

Wrapped in my camelhair rug
I'm camouflaged
out here in the desert.
My feet make no sound on the sand.
The sky is crawling with stars.

I shout, and it echoes
all the way to the sea.
No answering cry comes back to me.
I could be the last boy,
I could be up on the moon.

Nothing but flat for miles,
the occasional bone
strewn on the sand.
I take one back with me
to help bury my parachute.

I check my compass
and head due south-east.
A light wind covers my footprints.
I have no need of water.
I'll hit the oasis by dawn.

Matthew Sweeney

Auntie's Snake Cake

Auntie baked a birthday cake
for Albertine, her garter snake.
She mixed in worms, with slugs and snails
and frozen mice, complete with tails.
She beamed as Uncle stole a slice,
took a bite and said, "That's nice."

Marian Swinger

Computer Game

WHAM! WHAM! Zappa zappa!
Zappa zappa zoom!
There's a manic computer game
up in my room.

As soon as I switch off
the lamp every night
enemy space ships
appear on the right:

ZOOP-ZOOP! ZOOP-ZOOP!
Beep-beep-beep.
The noises it makes
stop me going to sleep.

Now as the main
invasion fleet nears
I snug in my pillow
with plugs in my ears.

ZAPOW! ZAP! ZAP-ZAP!
ZAP! POW-POW!
As you may have guessed,
I'm wide awake now.

Zip-zip! Zeep-zeep!
Zip! BAM-BAM!
The rockets rush,
the lasers slam,

the deck guns splat,
the ray guns blast,
each invader explodes
as it rushes past.

Bip-bip, bip-bip,
zeep-zeep ZAM!
Just one to go – look out!
BAM! BAM!

My ship is moving
in the deep.
Beep-beep, beep-beep,
beep beep beep.

The sky is black,
my ship is steady;
I open my eyes –
it's morning already!

Charles Thomson

Bony's Song

I'm long. I'm lean.
My skin is green.
My teeth are clean.
My grin is mean.
But mine is not a proper smile.
It's built of bitterness and bile.
And I have got a grim profile
cos I am not a nice reptile.
I'm Bony, Bony, Bony, Bony,
Bony Crocodile.

It's my delight
To pick a fight.
I'm dynamite.
I claw. I bite.
No, friendliness is *not* my style.
I play it cool but, all the while,
I'm actually very volatile
cos I am not a nice reptile.
I'm Bony, Bony, Bony, Bony,
Bony Crocodile.

My jaws are wide,
So slide inside.
We'll take a ride,
A snake-like glide,
A mile or two along the Nile.
I'll leave your bones there, in a pile.
Don't pull a face. You know I'm vile
cos I am not a nice reptile.
I'm Bony, Bony, Bony, Bony,
Bony Crocodile.

Nick Toczek

The Wart Hog

The tiger wouldn't change his stripes
Nor the leopard change a spot,
But if the wart hog had a choice,
He'd change the flipping lot.

John Turner

The Jumping Game

We jump the rope
We jump in line
We jump up high
We jump in time
We jump for luck
We jump again
We jump along
The jumping game.

We jump in ones
We jump in twos
We jump the lights
We jump the queues
We jump for joy
We jump again
We jump along
The jumping game.

We jump and fall
We jump and learn
We jump and twist
We jump and turn
We jump for kicks
We jump again
We jump along
The jumping game.

We jump for gold
We jump for free
We jump from A
We jump to B
We jump for fun
We jump again
We jump along
The jumping game.

Steve Turner

It's Not Supposed to Work Like This!

She kissed her prince upon his lips
(Not what you'd call a snog)
Just *pecked him* with her cupid lips
But turned him to a frog!

Philip Waddell

After School

we wait all day
for after school
for the bell to go
for the chairs to be stacked
for the chalk dust to settle
when the teachers relax
for the pell mell
helter skelter
race for the gates
where the gangs all wait
to settle old scores
conker fights
and nosebleeds
and wild bully roars
then the games of chain-chase
till the sun starts to dip
turn to catch-the-girl
kiss-the-girl
quick as quick
winding home past the sweet shop
for penny chews
where the paper boys huddle
to take out the news
till dawdling back alleys
and grim-fingered trees
lead us shadowing slowly
home for our teas

Dave Ward

Pulsation

Stomp to the rhythm.
Bomp to the beat.
Drum with your fingers.
Strut with your feet.

Thump with a broomstick.
Ding that brass.
Rap those railings.
Ping that glass.

Stomping rhythm.
Bomping beat.
Drumming fingers.
Strutting feet.

Whisk up a whisper
With sand in a tin.
Clash those pan-lids,
Make a real din.

Stomp to the rhythm.
Bomp to the beat.
Drum those fingers.
Feel the heat.

Pam Wells

Socks

My local Gents' Outfitter stocks
The latest line in snazzy socks:
Black socks, white socks,
Morning, noon and night socks,
Grey socks, green socks,
Small, large and in between socks,
Blue socks, brown socks,
Always-falling-down socks,
Orange socks, red socks,
Baby socks and bed socks;
Purple socks, pink socks,
What-would-people-think socks,
Holey socks and frayed socks,
British Empire-made socks,
Long socks, short socks,
Any-sort-of-sport socks,
Thick socks, thin socks,
And "these-have-just-come-in" socks.

Socks with stripes and socks with spots,
Socks with stars and polka dots,
Socks for ankles, socks for knees,
Socks with twelve-month guarantees,
Socks for aunties, socks for uncles,
Socks to cure you of carbuncles,
Socks for nephews, socks for nieces,
Socks that won't show up their creases,
Socks whose colour glows fluorescent,
Socks for child or adolescent,
Socks for ladies, socks for gents,
Socks for only fifty pence.

Socks for winter, socks for autumn,
Socks with garters to support 'em.
Socks for work and socks for leisure,
Socks hand-knitted, made-to-measure,
Socks of wool and polyester,
Socks from Lincoln, Leeds and Leicester,
Socks of cotton and elastic,
Socks of paper, socks of plastic,
Socks of silk-embroidered satin,
Socks with mottoes done in Latin,
Socks for soldiers in the army,
Socks to crochet or macramé,
Socks for destinations distant,
Shrink-proof, stretch-proof, heat-resistant.

Baggy socks, brief socks,
Union Jack motif socks,
Chequered socks, tartan socks,
School or kindergarten socks,
Sensible socks, silly socks,
Frivolous and frilly socks,
Impractical socks, impossible socks,
Drip-dry machine-only-washable socks,
Bulgarian socks, Brazilian socks,
There seem to be over a million socks!

With all these socks, there's just one catch –
It's hard to find a pair that match.

Colin West

My Sister Alexandra

My sister Alexandra
is a twister and a slanderer.
She tells on me, she fibs and spies,
gets me grounded by her lies.

My sister is a serpent,
stealthy, sly and slick.
Her tongue is sharp as scissors;
there's venom in her spit.

My sister is a wicked witch,
casting curse on curse.
She tricks and taunts and tortures –
but my *other* sister's worse!

Kate Williams

Blue Morning

after Terry Frost
for Kate Brindley

soft slap
blue lap
salt flap

of water
on wood
on water

cold sea
knocking

old boat
rocking

the salt slap
wave tap
blue map

new gap

of morning

Anthony Wilson

My Grandad

My Grandad
is a maniac.

He uses
the wrong side
of the road.

He parks
where he shouldn't.

He never signals . . .

I sometimes think
he shouldn't be allowed out
on that skateboard.

                    Bernard Young

I Luv Me Mudder

I luv me mudder an me mudder luvs me
We cum so far from over de sea,
We heard dat de streets were paved wid gold
Sometimes it's hot, sometimes it's cold,
I luv me mudder an me mudder luvs me
We try fe live in harmony
Yu might know her as Valerie
But to me she's just my mummy.

She shouts at me daddy so loud sometime
She's always been a friend of mine
She's always doing de best she can
She works so hard down ina Englan,
She's always singin sum kinda song
She has big muscles an she very, very strong,
She likes pussycats an she luvs cashew nuts
An she don't bother wid no if an buts.

I luv me mudder an me mudder luvs me
We come so far from over de sea,
We heard dat de streets were paved wid gold
Sometimes it's hot, sometimes it's cold,
I luv her and whatever we do
Dis is a luv I know its true,
My people, I'm talking to yu
Me an my mudder we luv yu too.

Benjamin Zephaniah

My Granny

Some grannies are knitters, some grannies make hats
Some grannies smoke kippers, some grannies keep cats
Some grannies have gardens and some live in flats
But my Granny's a lumberjack
How about that!

She never stays in on a Saturday night
She goes to the woods on her big mountain bike
And she chops down the trees with a thud and a thwack
Cos my Granny's a lumberjack
How about that!

The neighbours all think that my Granny is bonkers
She goes to the forest to rummage for conkers
Then she gets out her buzz-saw and suddenly CRACK!
Cos my Granny's a lumberjack
How about that!

She loves to go out when the weather is fine
And the sweet air is rich with the fresh smell of pine
As she clears up the forest with Chuck and Big Matt
Cos my Granny's a lumberjack
How about that!

Don't tell her she's old and don't tell her she's mad
Don't say all this dumb lumberjacking's a fad
Or she'll get out her buzz-saw and suddenly "SPLAT!"
Cos my Granny's a lumberjack
How about that!

Ann Ziety

Copyright Acknowledgments

The compiler and publishers would like to thank the
following for permission to reprint the selections
in this book:

John Agard for 'Secret'.
Jez Albrough for 'Ear Popping'.
Leo Aylen for 'The Recipe Alphabet'.
Gerard Benson for 'The Tale of the Leprechauny Man
    and the Unsuccessful Fishery Expedishery' from the
    Barrow Poets' *Christmas Howyahooha for Kids*.
James Berry for 'The Barkday Party', first published in
    When I Dance by Puffin Books.
Valerie Bloom for 'Whose Dem Boots'.
Margaret Blount for 'At the Hairdresser's'.
Stephen Bowkett for 'Love You Batman'.
Philip Burton for 'The Girl on the Touch Line'.
Dave Calder for 'Adding It Up', first published in *One
    In A Million* by Viking.
James Carter for 'Electric Guitars'.
Charles Causley for 'Family Album'.
Tony Charles for 'First Snow'.
Debjani Chatterjee for 'Diwali'.
John Coldwell for 'Help! Help! Walk For Your Lives!'.
Andrew Collett for 'How To Be Bad'.
Paul Cookson for 'The Spearmint Spuggy from Space
    Stuck on Every Seat in School'.
John Cooper Clarke for '(You Ain't Nothing But A)
    Hedgehog'.
Wendy Cope for 'Huff'.
Pie Corbett for 'Advice to an Ice Lolly Licker', first

published in *Another First Poetry Book* edited by
John Foster 1988.

Sue Cowling for 'Shocked'.

Ian Deal for 'Somewhere'.

Jan Dean for 'Their Secret is Out!'.

Peter Dixon for 'My Sister's Getting Married'.

Gina Douthwaite for 'This Kissing Business'.

Richard Edwards for 'The Shellfish Race', first published
in *A Mouse in My Roof* by Orchard/Puffin.

John Foster for 'Dad's Hiding in the Shed' from *Making
Waves* published by Oxford University Press.

Pam Gidney for 'Slug'.

Martin Glynn for 'Genius'.

Mick Gowar for 'Living Doll'.

Gus Grenfell for 'Who Is It?'.

Philip Gross for 'Nanny Neverley'.

Mike Harding for 'A Poem Called "Grown Ups Are Orl
Rite if Yoo Eat Them Hot"'.

David Harmer for 'There is Very Little Merit in a Ferret'.

Trevor Harvey for 'Favouritism', first published in
Poetry for Projects by Scholastic 1989.

John Hegley for 'The Emergensea'.

Stewart Henderson for 'No Trespassers'.

David Horner for 'Cake-Face'.

Libby Houston for 'All Change!' from *All Change*
published by Oxford University Press.

Ian McMillan for 'The Rhyming Bat'.

Mike Johnson for 'Something To Say'.

Jenny Joseph for 'Towards the End of Summer'.

Mike Jubb for 'Temper Temper'.

Jackie Kay for 'Word of a Lie'.

Jean Kenward for 'Tree and Leaf'.

Craig King for 'Are You There?'.

John Kitching for 'Lips'.

Tony Langham for 'When Mum Finally Went to Pieces'.

Anne Logan for 'Stock Cupboard Rap'.

Rupert Loydell for 'If You Were Made of Chocolate',
first published in *The Bees Sneeze* by Stride 1992.

Wes Magee for 'The Phantom's Fang-tastic Show'.

Linda Marshall for 'Close-Cropped Hair'.

Gerda Mayer for 'The Ice-Cream Poem' from *The
Knockabout Show* published by Chatto & Windus
1978. First published in the *New Statesman* 9
August 1958.

Kevin McCann for 'It is always the same dream'.

Roger McGough for 'Potato Clock', first published in
Sky in the Pie by Penguin. Reprinted by permission
of The Peters Fraser and Dunlop Group Limited.

Trevor Millum for 'Song of the Homeworkers', first
published in *Warning – Too Much Schooling Can
Damage Your Health* by Nelson.

Adrian Mitchell for 'Ode to my Nose', published in
Balloon Lagoon and the Magic Islands of Poetry by
Orchard Books 1997. Reprinted by permission of
The Peters Fraser and Dunlop Group Limited on
behalf of Adrian Mitchell. Educational Health
Warning! Adrian Mitchell asks that none of his
poems are used in connection with any examinations
whatsoever.

Tony Mitton for 'Make a Face'.

John Mole for 'The Invisible Man', from *The Dummy's
Dilemma* published by Hodder 1999.

Darren Moody for 'United Together'.

Marcus Moore for 'Limerick'.

Michaela Morgan for 'A to Z'.

Brian Moses for 'Bigfoot'.

Judith Nicholls for 'Have You Read . . . ?'. Reprinted by permission of the author.

Henry Normal for 'The Glaisdale Schoolyard Alliance of 1974'.

David Orme for 'Mr Kipling'.

Jack Ousbey for 'The Tent by the Sea'.

Gareth Owen for 'Bully'. Reprinted by permission of the author.

Brian Patten for 'Nasty Habit' from *The Utter Nutters* published by Penguin (Viking) 1994.

Andrew Fusek Peters for 'The Moon is on the Microphone', first published in *The Moon is on the Microphone – The Wild & Wacky Poems of Andrew Fusek Peters* by Sherbourne Publications 1987.

I.R. Eric Petrie for 'Mrs Thirkettle'.

Gervase Phinn for 'Interrogation in the Nursery'.

Simon Pitt for 'The Klorine Kid'.

Janis Priestley for 'But Of Course There Was Nobody There'.

Rita Ray for 'Break-Time Phrase Book'.

John Rice for 'Seaside Song' from *Zoomballoonballistic* published by Aten Press 1982.

Coral Rumble for 'When my Dad Watches the News', first published in *Baboons' Bottoms* by Initiative Press 1995.

Andrew Rumsey for 'Secret Affair'.

Anne Marie Sackett for 'Gecko'.

Vernon Scannell for 'My Dog'.

Fred Sedgwick for 'Auntie's Boyfriend', first published in *Blind Date* by Tricky Sam! Press.

Andrea Shavick for 'How To Successfully Persuade Your Parents To Give You More Pocket Money'.

Matt Simpson for 'When I Grow Up'.

Ian Souter for '999!'.
Roger Stevens for 'Treasure Trail'.
Matthew Sweeney for 'In the Desert'.
Marian Swinger for 'Auntie's Snake Cake'.
Charles Thomson for 'Computer Game'.
Nick Toczek for 'Bony's Song'.
John Turner for 'The Wart Hog'.
Steve Turner for 'The Jumping Game', from *The Day I Fell Down the Toilet* published by Lion 1996.
Philip Waddell for 'It's Not Supposed to Work Like This'.
Dave Ward for 'After School'.
Pam Wells for 'Pulsation'.
Colin West for 'Socks'. Reprinted with permission of the author.
Kate Williams for 'My Sister Alexandra'.
Anthony Wilson for 'Blue Morning' from *From Painting to Poem* published by Leamington Art Gallery and Museum.
Bernard Young for 'My Grandad', first published in *Penny Whistle Pete* by Collins 1995.
Benjamin Zephaniah for 'I Luv Me Mudder'.
Ann Ziety for 'My Granny', first published in *Bumwigs and Earbeetles and Other Unspeakable Delights* by Bodley Head 1995.

All possible care has been taken to trace the ownership of every selection included and to make full acknowledgement for its use. If any errors have accidentally occurred, they will be corrected in subsequent editions, provided notification is sent to the publishers.

Unzip Your Lips

100 Poems to Read Aloud chosen by Paul Cookson

100 poems to read aloud by 100 of the best modern poets from
Causley to Moses to Patten.

Out in the Desert

Out in the desert lies the sphinx
It never eats and it never drinks
Its body quite solid without any chinks
And when the sky's all purples and pinx
(As if it was painted with coloured inx)
And the sun it ever so swiftly sinx
Behind the hills in a couple of twinx
You may hear (if you're lucky) a bell that clinx
And also tolls and also tinx
And they say at the very same sound the sphinx
It sometimes smiles and it sometimes winx.

But nobody knows just what it thinx.

Charles Causley

Join In or Else

Poems for Joining In With chosen by Nick Toczek

A fantastic collection of poems to join in with, recite in class, say aloud with friends or even read on your own.

I Wrote Me a Poem

I wrote me some words and the words pleased me.
I told my words to the big oak tree.
My words went: "Jibber-jabber".
My song went: "Tree Shanty".
My limerick went: "Silly-billy".
My rhyme went: "Sky high".
My haiku went: "Slooooow thought."
My verse went: "Tickety-boo, tickety-boo".
My epic went: "Too long, much too long".
My ode went: "Lah . . . dah".
My sonnet went: "Oooh, love!"
My poem went: "Fiddle-eye-dee".

Bruce Barnes

The Works

Every kind of poem you will ever need for the Literacy Hour chosen by Paul Cookson

The Works really does contain every kind of poem you will ever need for the Literacy Hour but it is also a book packed with brilliant poems that will delight any reader.

It's got chants, action verses, riddles, tongue twisters, shape poems, puns, acrostics, haikus, cinquains, kennings, couplets, thin poems, lists, conversations, monologues, epitaphs, songs, limericks, tankas, nonsense poems, raps, narrative verse and performance poetry and that's just for starters.

It features poems from the very best classic and modern poets, for example:

William Blake, Michael Rosen, Robert Louis Stevenson, Allan Ahlberg, W. H. Auden, Brian Patten, Roger McGough, Roald Dahl, Charles Causley, Eleanor Farjeon, Benjamin Zephaniah, Ted Hughes, T. S. Eliot and William Shakespeare to name but a few.

A book packed with gems for dipping into time and time again.

Spill the Beans

An action-packed explosion of performance poems
by Paul Cookson and David Harmer

Meet Mr Moore the terrifying headmaster, join a picnic on the
M25, find out about the monster in the garden, listen to
the Tweaky Leaky Squeaky Brand New School Shoe Blues,
discover what lurks in a teacher's trouser turn-ups, uncover some
of the dinosaurs that time forgot and much much more.

Mister Moore

Mister Moore, Mister Moore
Creaking down the corridor.
Uh uh eh eh uh
Uh uh eh eh uh

Mister Moore wears wooden suits
Mister Moore's got great big boots
Mister Moore's got hair like a brush
And Mister Moore doesn't like me much.

Mister Moore, Mister Moore
Creaking down the corridor.

Uh uh eh eh uh
Uh uh eh eh uh

David Harmer

Let Me Touch the Sky

Selected poems for Children by Valerie Bloom

Let Me Touch the Sky is a brand-new selection of Valerie Bloom's warm, sparky and evocative poetry which will delight readers of all ages.

Autumn Gilt

The late September sunshine
Lime green on the linden leaves
Burns bronze on the slated roof-tops,
Yellow on the farmer's last sheaves.

It flares flame-like on the fire hydrant,
Is ebony on the blackbird's wing,
Blue beryl on the face of the ocean,
Glints gold on the bride's wedding ring.

A sparkling rainbow on the stained-glass window,
It's a silver sheen on the kitchen sink,
The late September sunshine
Is a chameleon, I think.

Valerie Bloom

A selected list of poetry books available from Macmillan

The prices shown below are correct at the time of going to press. However, Macmillan Publishers reserve the right to show new retail prices on covers which may differ from those previously advertised.

Unzip Your Lips
100 Poems to Read Aloud chosen by Paul Cookson
0 330 37062 6
£4.99

Join In or Else
Poems for joining in with, chosen by Nick Toczek
0 330 48263 7
£2.99

The Works
Chosen by Paul Cookson
0 330 48104 5
£4.99

Spill the Beans
Poems by Paul Cookson and David Harmer
0 330 39214 X
£3.99

Let Me Touch the Sky
Selected poems for children by Valerie Bloom
0 333 780671
£9.99

Mini Beasts
Poems chosen by Brian Moses
0 330 37057 X
£2.99

Ridiculous Relatives
Poems chosen by Paul Cookson
0 330 37105 3
£2.99

All Macmillan titles can be ordered at your local bookshop or are available by post from:

**Book Service by Post
PO Box 29, Douglas, Isle of Man IM99 1BQ**

Credit cards accepted. For details:
Telephone: 01624 675137
Fax: 01624 670923
E-mail: bookshop@enterprise.net

Free postage and packing in the UK.
Overseas customers: add £1 per book (paperback)
and £3 per book (hardback).